T0128577

DISTINCT ARROWS

Tonia Johnson

WESTBOW
PRESS®
A DIVISION OF THOMAS NELSON
& ZONDERVAN

WestBow Press books may be ordered through booksellers or by contacting:

WestBow Press
A Division of Thomas Nelson & Zondervan
1663 Liberty Drive
Bloomington, IN 47403
www.westbowpress.com
1 (866) 928-1240

ISBN: 978-1-9736-8023-9 (sc)
ISBN: 978-1-9736-8024-6 (hc)
ISBN: 978-1-9736-8022-2 (e)

Library of Congress Control Number: 2019918685

Print information available on the last page.

WestBow Press rev. date: 12/20/2019

CONTENTS

Preface ix

Acknowledgments xiii

Introduction xvii

Chapter 1 Building a Solid Foundation 1

Chapter 2 Identity and Affirmation 11

Chapter 3 Establishing Their Futures 21

Chapter 4 Finding Balance 39

Chapter 5 Diminishing Stereotypes 49

Chapter 6 Finishing Touches 63

Chapter 7 Legacy 71

Notes 77

About the Author 81

PREFACE

The Author's Heart

It is my prayer and intent to get this book into the hands of as many mothers, fathers, grandparents, aunts, uncles, foster parents, and caregivers as possible. As a mother of young adults, I am very grieved by the plight of our generations to come. As I write, our children are now twenty and twenty-six, so I understand the journey of raising children. It is my hope that those occupationally overworked parents and those who do not enjoy reading will find this book easy to finish and obtain knowledge.

Often, it is not an easy journey, but the decisions we make as parents have direct impacts on the futures of our children. I believe that parenting is rewarding and that children are gifts from God.

Mothers and fathers are blessed with the gift and beauty of a child, but I want to speak to mothers first because I am one. Mothers are responsible for caring for their children from conception. Fathers who decide to raise their children jointly or as a single parent are a great blessing. I also want to acknowledge grandmothers, aunts, cousins, and others who have stepped in to rescue family members who may have struggled with the idea of being a parent.

There are times when I have erred because I was in the learning process of motherhood. I have learned and accepted correction from my heavenly Father through His Word. I have repented often, have asked my children for forgiveness, and have sought wisdom because I have wanted to become better.

Many times, the way we parent has been passed down to us from generation to generation. We find that we are not in line with the Word of God. In this day and age, there is a generation of mothers who was not parented properly due to drug addiction, abandonment, or a refusal to accept guidance from someone who was older and wiser.

I ask that you hear the cries of your children speaking through these pages. I pray that these pages will illuminate before you and that your eyes will see, your ears will hear, and your heart will receive the wisdom of God found in them.

ACKNOWLEDGMENTS

Thank You, my God and my Father in heaven who pushed me. Thank You, Jesus, my Lord and Savior! You are always faithful to me. I willingly render you glory, honor, and majesty.

To my firstborn and my second-born children, who lovingly refer to yourselves, I tell you every chance I get that I love you and will say it again because I want the world to know it too; "I love *you* so very much." Thank you for loving, forgiving, and giving my own words of wisdom back to me when necessary. In whatever I was assigned to do in that time and season, you both always stood with me and cheered for me. You have encouraged and at times pushed me to complete this book.

To the father of my children, who has been my husband for over three decades and is the smartest man I know, I thank you for your many sacrifices. I truly love you. I am grateful for your massive support and guidance with every requirement of this project. We have had some great highs with a view from the top of the mountains. We have also absolutely encountered some tumultuous lows. Together, we are still standing.

Thanks to L. Thompson, whom I have never forgotten. It was during a deployment for our family that you repeatedly told me that our son was going to be all right. You believed in him.

You sowed love into his life. For this, I am grateful.

Thanks to A. Johnson and R. Hunte for your relentless, faithful prayers, which have covered me, and for interceding on my behalf. I am grateful for your sound, godly wisdom and loyal friendship.

To K. Johnson with much gratitude! Without hesitation, you provided a valuable resource.

N. Finklea, thank you for your patience throughout this process and for your professional guidance.

INTRODUCTION

Don't you see that children are God's best gift?
The fruit of the womb his generous legacy? Like
a warrior's fistful of arrows are the children of a
vigorous you. Oh, how blessed are you parents,
with your quivers full of children! (Psalm
127:3–5 MSG)

The *Oxford English Dictionary* describes
the word *arrow*[1] as a weapon that consists of a
thin, straight stick with a sharp point, which is

designed to be shot from a bow. It also describes an arrow as a mark or a sign that resembles an arrow and is used to show direction or position.

This source also defines the word *distinct*[2] as something that is recognizably different in nature from something else and is readily distinguishable by the senses. My definition would be that it is *noticeably identified*.

Distinct Arrows is a source to assist parents and caregivers in directing their children in confident and productive ways through every stage of their childhoods and into their adult lives. This book offers you guidance as you position your children in their place on the landscape of life.

CHAPTER 1

Building a Solid
Foundation

———◆———

Your children are gifts from God, no matter
how they were conceived. Conception may have
happened because two married people mutually
agreed on it, out of wedlock, because of rape,
or by an adulterous relationship. God allowed
that baby to be conceived in the womb, and

according to Psalm 127:3 (KJV), he or she is a reward from Him. God says, "Before I formed you in the womb I knew you; and before you were born I approved of you" (Jeremiah 1:5 ERV). That baby is already set apart for a special work. God has planned something great for him or her to do on the earth.

Your role as a parent can determine whether your child will get the opportunity to do a special work and make a difference in this world. During the developmental stages, your child will be a great responsibility to you. Your child will need to be nurtured and guided by a loving adult and will have other needs. I summon you to fulfill your responsibility as a parent. Your child is worth the sacrifice.

Often shortly after their births, children are dedicated to God through baptismal ceremonies or pastoral blessings. This dedication is parents bringing their children before their pastors to be blessed by God. Pastors and some ministers are ordained to do so. However, there are children who have not been dedicated to God. My hope is that you consult with your pastor and allow him to bless your child.

If your child has not been dedicated, and you do not have a church, I stand with you today, as an ordained minister of the gospel of Jesus Christ, to bless your child. Please pray the following prayer, replacing the blanks with your child's name:

> Father God, we lift _____ up to You. We give _____ back to You as You gave _____to us. _____ is Yours. We ask You to bless _____ . We ask You to take care of _____. We ask You teach _____ who You are. As parents, we have decided to make a conscientious effort to raise _____ in a way that will be pleasing to You. Forgive us for not knowing the best way.

> Dear God, we ask You to show us how to take care of _____. We have decided to ask You and to seek godly counsel from our pastor, a social worker, our family members, and friends who have made You first in their lives, regarding those things we do not know. We commit to do better by praying, learning about You, and finding a church that will teach us how to lead our family. In Jesus' name, amen.

And the child grew and became strong in spirit, filled with wisdom; and the grace of God was upon Him. (Luke 2:40 MEV)

Teach your children who God is very early in their lives. Proverbs 22:6 says, "Dedicate your children to God and point them in the way that they should go, and the values they've learned from you will be with them for life" (TPT). Teach them to pray. Incorporating regular church attendance and fellowship into your schedule will nurture your child and offer guidance and support to you. Your child will learn of God, and you will be taught the things you never knew.

Our society has deliberately decided to raise children outside of the belief in the Almighty God. This decision has led to lawlessness and disrespect for the authorities who have been put in place to protect them, such as teachers, adults, and even you as the parent. Jesus Christ, the Son of God, said that the little children should not be kept from coming to Him because the kingdom of heaven belonged to those who were like them (see Matthew 19:14–15 ERV).

Don't worry that your child will be a distraction during a church service. He may cry, play, or fall asleep, but your child is learning. A May 10, 2017, University of Colorado, Boulder, study said "What an infant hears during sleep has an immediate and profound impact on his or her brain activity, potentially shaping language learning later in life"[3] (Gilley 2017).

Your child may be asleep during church service, but he or she is processing information about the acoustic environment. Your child's brain is using the information to develop pathways for learning.

The study goes on to say that the baby's brain quickly learned certain sounds and reacted with surprise to different ones. Because your children can learn language and sounds when they are asleep, they can also hear and receive the Word of God while in church or at a Bible study. Do not leave your child at home when you go to church; even if you will be busy serving in some compacity as well. You may feel that it is an inconvenience to bring your children, but it is worth it.

It was very rare for our children to stay home from church. I was not easily convinced to let them stay home because of sickness or having too much homework, as they grew older. I actually observed that their grades were better during times when the church had more events. When children are left alone, they are prone to watch television, play video games, or look at items on the Internet that impose on their innocence.

God loves you and your child. We are His creations. I invite you to communicate with Him and to teach your child to talk to God as well. It will bless the life of your child. Prayer is merely talking to God.

The disciples, whom Jesus had called to follow Him, asked Him how they should pray.

> "And he said unto them, when ye pray, say, our Father which art in heaven, Hallowed be thy name. Thy kingdom come. Thy will be done, as in heaven, so in earth. Give us day by day our daily bread. And forgive us our sins; for we also forgive every

one that is indebted to us. And lead us not into temptation; but deliver us from evil." (Luke 11:1–4 KJV)

Teach your children to always be grateful and to give thanks daily to God Almighty. It is my prayer that your children will always have a place to live and that there will always be food in your home. I am believing with you for their school tuitions, scholarships, and that uniforms will be accessible. Trust God.

Dear Mama, How Much Money Is This?

I am amazed at the number of students and teenagers working in restaurant chains with big names and in drive-through coffee shops who do not know how to count money. It is quite disturbing. Not so long ago, there was a time when children were required to know how to expeditiously count money and distribute change. They had to know how to break down the bills and the coins.

Have you ever been in a situation where you realized that you had the exact change after the cashier had already closed the cash register? You try to give the attendant the exact amount and get a look like a deer seeing headlights. Sometimes the attendant says, "I have already entered the amount in the register." This is when the cashier can show whether or not he or she can count money in his or her head and not rely on the machine.

We need our children to be critical and creative thinkers, not only computer operators. Will we just accept what a computer determines? Our children need to know how to manage their personal lives as well. I always emphasized to our children the importance of knowing how to count money so that they would not be cheated or receive incorrect change after a transaction.

CHAPTER 2

Identity and Affirmation

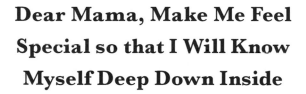

Dear Mama, Make Me Feel Special so that I Will Know Myself Deep Down Inside

Although they may not yet understand it, your children need to know that they are princes and princesses. Do you know that when you accept Jesus Christ as Lord and Savior, and live honorably for Him; you, your children, and your family are part of the royal priesthood of God? First Peter 2:9 says, "But you are a chosen race, a royal priesthood, a holy nation, a people for his own possession, that you may proclaim the excellencies of him who called you out of darkness into his marvelous light" (NASB).

Your expressions, touches, and exhortations will establish who your children are meant to be. Your children will not know this if you throw profane words at them and are constantly swearing. Your children will eventually mimic you, and it will cause you embarrassment.

We learn our disciplinary skills from the way our parents or caregivers treated us. Beating your child in anger and throwing your child around without regard are violent behaviors. As parents, we are to discipline our children without harming them and to steer them properly.

We have heard that "the rod and reproof give wisdom, but a child who is left to himself brings shame to his parents" (see Proverbs 29:15). I am not an advocate of time-outs on a chair as discipline. In most instances, the child does not stay on the chair, which can cause the parent's temper to escalate. You can begin with a warning for the child to stop the action. If your child does not display immediate correction for the behavior, taking away a toy your child enjoys or withholding a freedom can be alternative discipline. If these examples fail, your child may need love demonstrated by a harmless spanking.

We have also heard that "the parent who spares the rod hates his or her child, but the parent who loves the child diligently disciplines him" (see Psalm 13:24). We are to have the same love for our children that Jesus Christ has for them. If you find this difficult, seek counseling, allow a trusted friend or relative to relieve you, or consider allowing those who would like to parent to adopt your child.

Your children need to know who they are. Psalm 139:14 says that "God has fearfully and wonderfully made you through His marvelous works." Your children will need your endless love and your time invested into their lives.

Dear Mama, Please Protect Me

I plead with you not to leave your children with strangers, those who are new friends, or all relatives and neighbors. They may not be as nice as they have led you to believe. Some of these people might hurt or violate your children. Daily, we see through the news media and from cell phone alerts that our world is full of dangerous people living among good people who are focused on living as they were intended to.

According to the Office of Juvenile Justice and Delinquency Prevention, "in 2018, there were four hundred twenty-four thousand sixty-six reports of missing persons involving youth, entered into the Federal Bureau of Investigations, National Crime Information Center (NCIC). A total of 612,846 missing persons reports was submitted to NCIC, of those 85,459 records remained active as of December 31, 2018. Youth accounted for 34.8 percent of those active missing person records"[4] (OJJDP, 2019). These statistics are not intended to make you fearful but to cause you to guard, watch, and pray over your child.

I love the Bible passage that describes Jesus asking the disciples if they could just stay up and watch as He prayed. They were his followers and friends. He was their teacher. We are to follow Christ's example and to lead our children as Jesus instructed us to. Jesus said, "Keep actively watching and praying that you may not come into temptation" (Matthew 26:41 AMP). We can hopefully stop predators when we do this.

Dear Mama, I Am So Confused

"Whoever causes one of these little ones who believe in me to sin, it would be better for him if a great millstone were hung around his neck and he were thrown into the sea". (Mark 9:42 ESV)

We must break the chain of family secrets and the cycle of sexual abuse. Hosea 4:6 says, "My people are destroyed for lack of knowledge" (KJV).

Not one uncle, grandfather, aunt, cousin, babysitter, or father should be left unaccountable for violating a child. Whether it is molestation or rape, it is an offense. These are selfish and demonic acts. They are also generational and come from ancestral curses.

The Bible says, "keeping mercy for thousands, forgiving iniquity and transgression and sin, and that will by no means clear the guilty; visiting the iniquity of the fathers upon the children, and upon the children's children, unto the third and to the fourth generation" (Exodus 34:7 KJV).

Often children are molested and raped by the very people that you have taught them to trust. This is when many seeds are planted, which can destroy a child's life. It can even confuse them of their sexual orientation.

God never makes mistakes! This is an attack from Satan himself. Because God created human beings, they should be subject to Almighty God. Therefore, they should be under submission to Him and not controlled by their flesh. Our minds, emotions, and hearts should be spiritually healthy. Colossians 3:5

says, "Put to death therefore what is earthly in you: sexual immorality, impurity, passion, evil desire, and covetousness, which is idolatry" (MEV).

Dear Mama, Believe Me When I Tell You What They Did to Me

If your child tells you that someone has touched him or her inappropriately, you should believe your child unless it is determined otherwise. It is important to be so engaged with your child that you will know if his or her behavior is abnormal. Allow your child to come to you. Always let your child know that he or she can talk to you about anything and that you will listen to, believe, and defend him or her.

Psalm 138:7 tells us that "although we walk in the midst of trouble, God will preserve our lives, stretch out His hand against the wrath of our enemies, and deliver us". Thousands of years ago, there was a wicked king, who was called a pharaoh. He absolutely hated God's chosen people, the Israelites. They were living in another country, which was called Egypt. Although the Egyptians oppressed them, they were very productive. The women gave birth to many children, and therefore, the Israelites multiplied.

Pharaoh did not like this fact and decreed that all Israeli male babies should be killed. One Israelite mom and dad were determined to save their son's life. "By faith, they hid him for three months because they saw he was a beautiful child and they were not afraid of the king's edict" (see Hebrews 11:23). The baby boy's mother placed him in a basket among the reeds of the Nile River.

The basket could have turned over and drowned the baby. He could've been eaten by the great creatures of the Nile. However, the baby's sister watched over him and wondered what would happen to her brother. I believe his parents knew that God Almighty would protect and save their son, and He did.

The phenomenal part about this true story is that this very baby boy, named Moses, many years later, was instructed by God to stand before pharaoh and to demand the Israelites' freedom from slavery. He helped set the Israelites free from over four hundred years of slavery. There is a mighty plan for your child's life as well.

CHAPTER 3

Establishing
Their Futures

———⟫◆⟪———

Dear Mama, Prepare
Me for School

Teach your child the alphabet, numbers, and
shapes. Teach them how to write their names
before they start primary school. Demonstrate

in front of them how to listen and to follow the directions of adults and teachers. They need to understand what yes and no mean before they enter school. Your children must know how to follow directions and to be good listeners. If they learn this first at home, they will not be constant distractions or labeled as a "problem child" by the educational system.

At an early age, you should teach your child the importance of learning and education. Before your child leaves your presence, please pray with and over him or her:

- For God Almighty's protection
- That your child will be obedient to all who are in charge
- That your child will learn all that his or her teachers place before him or her

What to Pray

Father God, I ask You to give this beautiful child self-control and patience so that my child can sit and learn for an extended length of time. I pray that my child will stay focused during instruction each day. I pray that the teacher will extend care toward my child and that the environment will be peaceful. I pray that my child will respect his/her peers and that his/her peers will respect my child. In Jesus' name, amen.

Dear Mama, Read to Me

Read, read, and read! I believe that giving a book to a small child so that he or she can hold it cultivates and stimulates that child's desire to read. Reading can unlock a child's imagination and stimulate creativity. Reading takes a child on a journey to adventure. Reading gives hope. Reading will inspire a child to dream.

During my childhood, in one of my books, a girl named Heidi took me away from my environment. I don't know if I ever thought about going to Switzerland, but in my forties, I did. I was overjoyed. As I stood at the highest elevation in the Alps of Switzerland, I remembered those books about Heidi and was overcome with emotion. Our children wondered what was wrong with me, but I remembered my life's journey. Growing up in a broken and dysfunctional house can make it difficult to dream. At times, all you have is a dream. Somehow those Heidi books collided with a fifth grade social studies series. I distinctly remember learning all the continents, their countries, and the cultural significance for many of them. This allowed me to escape far away from the life I was living day to day. Reading broadens your horizons, expands your perspectives, and creates an interest in you for other places in the world.

I gave books as gifts to our children. We frequently visited bookstores. I believe our son had to start wearing glasses because he always read books by flashlight under the covers in bed when he should have been asleep. Both of our children continue to tell me about fascinating things they have learned from reading.

Dear Mama, Come to My School to See What I Am Learning and Help My Teacher When You Can

Before you send your child off to school, instill in them the importance of listening to their teachers. This includes respecting their teachers.

Recently, during a conversation with a previous coworker whom I had worked with outside of the United States, she reminded me of my words. Each morning, she heard me say to my children, "Be a good listener." When she became a grandmother and helped with her grandchild's caregiving, she told me that she started telling her grandchild what she had heard me say daily to my children. You never know who is listening and what impact you will have on others, whether it is positive or negative.

If you allocate just a little time (a lunch hour or a day off from work) to visit your child at school, you can help change his or her negative outlook on school or encourage your child to achieve greater things. Often, young children want to show off their moms or dads to their teachers or friends. They are proud that you are their parent.

We should always show respect toward our children's teachers. Your child should never see you yelling or using profane language toward a teacher or a principal. It is not advisable to talk about the teacher or staff negatively at home in the hearing of your children. The teachers, principal, and school staff need your support.

I encourage you to find out about any concern that the teacher has for your child with his or her academics and/or discipline. We must realize that the child will attempt to treat his teacher the same way he sees you treating that teacher. Please make it your goal to teach your child to respect teachers and other school administrators.

There are no quick fixes. Some children have been clinically diagnosed and need assistance to learn. Some children need medications. We truly need to use caution when using these long-term medications. If your child is prescribed medication, I recommend you obtain clarity of understanding for the medications and their long-term effects. As their parent, believe your child can learn. In addition, be mindful of strong school documentation and unfortunate labeling of the child.

Our son was involved in a bullying situation. One day after school, he was attacked right in our housing community, after getting off the bus. As a result, the principal decided our son needed to see a Child Psychologist and possibly be medicated although our son was attacked. She decided our son could not return to school otherwise. We strongly believed; the principal was punishing our son for being a victim. I went through this very painful journey. I did not want to comply because I knew nothing was wrong with our son. Due to my husband's profession, we felt that it was best to follow through with the principal's request. Our son continuously asked me not to put him on the medication. He said, "There is nothing wrong with me." It was such a difficult and complex situation. He was an eighth grader, and I had to give him the medication and watch him take it each morning. Each day I would hear him say,

"Mom there is nothing wrong with me." This definitely made me feel bad.

One day while his dad was away, my son begged me to allow him to stop the medication. He told me that he would prove nothing was wrong with him. I was hesitant yet agreed to his request. I was active in his life, observed his progress, and covered him with lots of prayer. Our son never took the medication again.

I am not saying our son was a perfect child. He wanted to be active and became bored easily if the subject matter did not grab his attention. There were highs and lows. He would stay up all night to complete an assignment and then leave it at home. He would miss the bus regularly, and the drive to his school was an hour long.

At other times, he would say to me, "I am not going back to football, and I am not staying after school for practice."

My response would be, "You better not come home on the early bus." He understood exactly what I meant. It was during times like these that I had to parent hard. Despite some of the challenges, our son continued to improve each school year in academics and sports.

In high school, he earned a team-captain position and placed well in wrestling. He also worked with the British staff at his international school. The counselor and principal told me how well the staff liked him and that they were not easy to please.

Every minute, a child can be born with life-threatening, incurable diseases. Unfortunately, a newborn baby may not be released from the hospital with the mother. He or she may require specific treatments or corrective surgery. Some diseases occur in various stages after birth and can be linked to vaccinations. Diagnoses have been made following extended examinations. In some findings, these diagnoses are autism, asthma, and ADHD (attention-deficit/hyperactivity disorder).

I believe there is a need for vaccinations. Vaccinations help prevent diseases. If your child is diagnosed with one of these, I encourage you to educate yourself about the diagnosis and to believe God for your child's healing, good health, and the wisdom of how to care for your child.

When our daughter was in high school, I spoke with her guidance counselor regularly to ensure that she was on track for college. During one conversation, I shared how I had been concerned about my son doing well at his new college. After my son had determined his interest of study, I had noticed that he did better at the university level than at previous schools. Our daughter's counselor shared that highly intelligent children can struggle more in school if subjects do not interest them.

Our son graduated from university with honors. He would often call and share the intriguing information that he was learning. He earned a bachelor of arts degree in English with a minor in international relations. He previously worked as a supervisor at a learning center. Now he is an English teacher in China. He is preparing to begin coursework for a master's degree. To God be all the glory forever.

Dear Mama, Celebrate My Achievements at Every Stage

I believe that all children can learn. I believe that children only determine that they cannot solve a math problem or complete a project if they say they cannot. Encourage and quietly pray for your child so that he or she will get the correct answers and successfully complete projects. Whether I observed for myself or learned through the teacher that our children were having difficulties in areas of study, I never told them that they wouldn't be able to do the work.

We must be careful what we say to our children. If we tell them, "I was never good at math, so this is why you are having problems," this allows doubt to creep in and diminishes their self-confidence. Instead, reinforce what the teacher is teaching. Workbooks are available at bookstores and budget-friendly stores as well. There are online and after-school tutoring programs. Speaking life to the area of difficulty, such as, "You can do it," "You are very smart," and "I am so proud of you," can change their outcomes. Your children will know that you believe in them and will gain confidence to try harder to figure out the process. During your own prayer time and when you pray with your child, ask God to give your child knowledge and understanding in the areas of concern. Watch God give your child what he or she needs to excel in that area.

I tend to ask those I am in personal and professional relationships, how their children are doing. I ask because I genuinely care. I listen to the frustrations that they share with the knowledge that parenting is not easy. I want them to understand that parenting is not easy but that in the midst of their circumstances, parenting is also a blessing.

When I was three months pregnant with our daughter, a specialist told me that she would not develop the way she should. I was shocked and devastated. God gave us a miracle. I am forever grateful. I delivered a very good, easy child. She was interested in learning. She went to day care and then to preschool.

At the end of her kindergarten year, her teacher wanted to retain her. I was not against it because she was a *young kindergartener* (the term used for a child who starts school when he or she is four years old and will turn five during the school year). I was also concerned that if we moved to a new school district, she might be held back because of her age (based on different district guidelines). I verbally agreed with the teacher but did not sign the paperwork.

The teacher's assistant came to me very upset

and said, "I will not allow you to do this to my baby. There are other students being promoted who do not know as much as she does. She can and will learn." I decided that I would not allow our daughter to be held back.

By the time she was in second grade, her teacher said, "Do everything I tell you to do with your daughter." I was working outside of the home full-time, but I was determined to do everything her teacher told me to do. She did very well throughout the school year.

We moved just before her third grade. Her teacher wanted her to excel as well. Again, I did everything the teacher instructed me to do and worked in the classroom regularly. When her teacher suggested speech therapy, I did not think she needed it but trusted the teacher's desire for our daughter's educational achievement.

Our daughter was on the honor roll throughout her years of schooling. She also earned the President's Education Award during the first year of Barak Obama's presidency. Right now, she is in her final year of college and continues to be recognized for high academic achievements. She amazes me. Today, I stand with you for your children and ask you to pray with them daily before they leave your home.

What to Pray

Dear Father, in the name of Jesus, anoint _____ with Your Spirit this day. Put a covering of protection all around my child. I ask that no hurt or harm may touch or come near my child. Father God, I ask that You always give _____ a way of escaping from any plan of Satan. I command that every scheme be cancelled right now in the name of Jesus. I ask You to send Your angels ahead of and with my child for all the days of his/her life.

I thank You for Your grace and mercy. I ask that You grant favor and kindness to my child with each teacher, principal, administrator, classmate, nurse, lunchroom worker, and custodian. Dear God, give_____ wisdom, knowledge, and understanding of every subject. As _____ finishes homework assignments and prepares for tests, I ask that You bring everything to his/her remembrance. Give my child peace during tests and assignments. Multiply the time allotted for my child to complete all the work that is before him/her. We thank You for a joyful, productive day. In Jesus name, amen.

CHAPTER 4

Finding Balance

———✦———

Dear Mama, Don't Be a Soccer Mom

It is probably not intentional, but parents boast or brag constantly about their children. Friendships should not be smothered by imposing competition. Neighbors and extended family members should not hate to see you coming. Healthy competition encourages growth in children and teaches them how to get along with others. This helps prepare them for life as adults in their professions.

However, allow your children to be children. Do not overextend your children with too many extracurricular activities, which can lead to depression and anxiety and result in their having difficulty balancing schoolwork and after-school activities. Please do not let your children suffer in their studies because you are trying to live out your dreams through your children. This is called *living vicariously through your child*. It means living out missed opportunities and failed dreams through your child. Doing so causes your child to feel that he or she must perform to earn your approval and ultimately, your love.

I have a very pleasant memory of our daughter participating in a youth tennis camp, which Wimbledon instructors led. The instructors suggested that she had potential, but she did not want to pursue tennis.

Not every child will be a professional football or baseball player, a doctor, or a billionaire. Allow your child to be an individual of good character and godly integrity and to be happy in whatever profession God calls them to serve.

I was strategic in establishing boundaries for our children concerning extracurricular activities. While living in Germany and later Belgium, sports and activities sometimes took our children on long journeys. It may have been a bus ride to England, crossing the English Channel by ferry, or a flight to Sicily. Our children would arrive home late on a Saturday night or at the break of day on a Sunday morning. I had great empathy for each of them and sometimes wanted to give in, allow them to sleep, and not attend church that day. However, I steadfastly believed that worship and the Word of God was far more integral to their well-being.

Jesus said, "It is written, Man shall not live by bread alone, but by every word that proceedeth out of the mouth of God" (Matthew 4:4 KJV). While teaching our children the words and instructions of God, we should make significant efforts to live out what we are saying we believe.

Often, the girl's organization, which our daughter was a member of, requested that she participate in activities on various Sundays during specific times of the year. In our home, the day set aside for our Sabbath day is Sunday. God told Moses to tell His people, "You must remember to keep the Sabbath a special day … But the seventh day is a day of rest in honor of the Lord your God" (see Exodus 20:8, 10 ERV).

I was not instilling a religious tradition but parenting and obeying God. I understood that one day my children would be adults living on their own. I am hopeful that they will nurture their own relationships with Jesus because they were taught and trained "not to worship any other gods except God" and "not to make idols" out of sports and other activities (Exodus 20:3–4 ERV).

It is true that parents sometimes give in a bit to the youngest child. This was true for us, especially because the youngest was a baby girl. I would remind myself that I had not allowed our son to skip a Sunday service and that he was now in college, boldly serving God. Therefore, I was hopeful that this same discipline would benefit our daughter as well.

Our son played youth basketball, soccer, and made a hole in one without effort during a golf camp, which surprised the instructors. We traveled to various communities with him for youth soccer. We traveled with him extensively during his high school years, when he played football and wrestled. While living in Germany, we bought airline tickets to meet his team in Italy. We would drive to Belgium and throughout Germany to support him.

He played well in football and made great accomplishments in wrestling. When he applied for the university of his choice, the college's coach talked with him during his visit about playing for the school's team. However, our son determined that he did not want to play football in college. Our son decided that he was more passionate about wrestling.

During high school, he tried out for wrestling at the request of a friend's mom. His friend was a football teammate. Football season was almost over when one evening after school, his friend's mom told my son to just go and check it out. Our son was not interested at all. He spent quite a bit of time at their house and respected their family.

Our son went to practice and was willing to give it a try. After a few practices, he started to like it. When he later understood the weight categories, the fear set in. For some reason, he believed that his opponent was bigger, based on his height. There was an exceptionally skilled, very tall, and totally muscular opponent who would always frighten my son when he had to wrestle him.

I knew that the Spirit that God gave us did not make us afraid. His Spirit is a source of power, love, and self-control (see 2 Timothy 1:7 ERV). I would prepare my son's diet as the coaches had advised. I constantly shared words of encouragement and motivation with our son. Whether he was on the football field and had to tackle the fiercest players or a gym floor, I would remind him of the story I had taught him about David and Goliath. I would tell him, "You are like David, and your opponent is Goliath." I would ask, "What did David do?" We agreed that David took down Goliath and so could my son.

This story is found in 1 Samuel 17. The

soldiers were filled with great fear of Goliath, but David stepped forward with confidence. David pulled a stone from his sling and threw it. With great force, it hit Goliath right in the middle of his forehead. That big giant, Goliath, fell forward and hit the ground dead. David ran to him, grabbed Goliath's sword, and cut off his head (see 1 Samuel 17:49–51 KJV).

When my son went to college, he soon began practicing with the school's wrestling team. One night, I received a call from him. I thought he was just calling to talk, but instead, he called asking where the nearest hospital was. He was attending school in my hometown, and the coach was not from the area. It was a startling phone call. He had sustained a major injury once before during high school.

He had to go through an agonizing rehabilitation process with a physical therapist, who was an expert in his field. Our son had an amazing recovery, so much so, that he placed third in his weight category for all of Europe's Department of Defense Dependents schools sports. To God be all the glory!

Now again, our son had to go through physical therapy as a result of another major injury. This ended his aspiration of wrestling in college. Life takes turns like a long, narrow, and winding road does.

Dear Mama, I Need Your Attention

How much time do you spend on your cell phone? Cell phones are a great convenience that can also control our lives. Children need our attention and interaction. They should never feel that they are an interruption to an ongoing conversation.

We should also ask ourselves how necessary it is for very young children to have their own cell phones. The entire car ride with your child, the drop-off and pickup for school or activities, and while in a restaurant or during dinner at home should not be regarded as the time for cell phone conversations. It saddens me to hear a mom or a dad say to the child, "Sit down and shut up," because he or she is casually talking on a cell phone.

The cell-phone phenomenon has hypnotized our society. It has made a difference in our lives by giving us access to communication whenever it is needed, but it has also moved us further away from interacting with our children.

CHAPTER 5

Diminishing Stereotypes

———◆———

Dear Mama, I Am
Afraid of the Police

I grew up around police officers, so I have respect for them. My father is a retired police officer. Often, we would ride in the back seat of his police car to school. My godfather was also an officer and my sister's godfather were a sheriff deputy. They also worked to full retirement as our dad did.

My father wasn't a perfect man. By the time I was eight years old, he no longer lived in our house. By the time I was ten, my parents had divorced. Even though this disappointed me, I still respected law enforcers.

I remember being shown stolen bicycles and even a jail cell. I was shown tough love. My father would say, "If you go to jail, I am not getting you out." In high school, I worked at our state capitol. Because I arrived at work later in the day, it was often difficult to find a place to park the car. I would get many parking tickets each month, and sometimes my car would be towed. At that point, most of my paycheck went to paying the tickets and recovering the car.

After I had paid a large number of tickets at the police station, someone suggested that I ask my father to have the tickets removed. I was very surprised. I could hardly wait to ask him. When I did, he said that he would not have the tickets removed. I was disappointed.

It wasn't until many years later in my adult life that I thanked him for not canceling the parking tickets. Police officers are there to enforce the laws that have been established for our nation. There has been great turmoil in our nation concerning law enforcement. Some concerns are very valid. Parents, please teach your children to respect the laws of our country, to be respectful to police officers, and to submit to their requests if a situation should ever arise.

We lived outside of the United States for many years. When our son was in high school, we lived in one country while our children attended school and participated in activities in a neighboring country. They rode a school bus one hour each way in and out of that country. Our son played sports and participated in Christian youth programs.

My husband and I attended a night event for his job. After the event, we drove to pick up our son from an event in the neighboring country. It was nearing midnight as we approached the border back into the country where we lived. Police officers stopped us. It was very frightening to be stopped in a foreign country.

The two policemen asked our son to get out of the car and instructed us to remain in the car. We did not know what would happen to our son. I watched them as they asked him a lot of questions. Our son remained calm throughout the questioning and was polite to both officers. After lengthy questioning, they allowed him to return to our car. We were so proud of him. He was able to stand under the pressure because we had taught him at a young age to respect all adults and all laws.

The law says that police officers have jurisdiction. Please teach your children to surrender to the requests of an officer. If there is ever a concern, you as the parent should handle it by submitting the necessary paperwork for a complaint.

It is my heartfelt prayer that your children will not be handled improperly by law enforcement officers. I pray that your children are never caught in the crossfire of a shooting. I pray that your children will be able to move to and from places with ease and without fear, as they live the lives God has given them. My prayer is that your children will always make the best decisions and will not become entangled with crime. I pray that the angels of the Lord will go before your children and will protect them. I pray that angels will guard them wherever they go: on playgrounds, at schools, or at sports events. Amen

Dear Mama, I Do Not Want to Be Unfairly Judged by Others

It is hurtful for a child to be judged unfairly. Use caution and judgement when determining what you want your child to have in life. Otherwise, they may grow up not wanting what you have attached to them. Please do not live out your fantasies through your child.

Ask yourself if your son really wants a pierced ear. Make him pull up his pants and wear a belt and do not allow his underwear to be seen. When I was fifteen, I thought that getting three piercings in my ear was cool; however, they did not have significance when I was thirty-something. I encourage you as the parent to dress your girl as the little girl she is.

We do not want to diminish the boundaries of your child, but it is important that your child does not think his or her worth is in his or her clothes or having the latest shoes. If your children feel that material possessions, the latest fashions, and looking good are important and required in order to be accepted, they can make wrong or bad decisions because of their desires to be validated or to fit in.

Dear Mama, Do Not Accept Government Assistance Unless We Really Need Help

Last year, I rethought my party affiliation. When I listened to the news and heard so much of what I did not agree with, I asked myself why I was letting this party represent me. I had become linked to the party because when I had needed to register to vote as a U.S. citizen, I had asked my parents what party they had been affiliated with. Each had told me which one and why. For more than thirty-five years, I was affiliated with the same party. It does not mean that at specific times and over the years, I did not think the party addressed my concerns, but as I evolved and increased my faith in God, I believed differently.

Unfortunately, there are bonds of poverty that plague families, generation after generation. Many people are tied to the welfare system. Others learn how to manipulate the system through friends. It becomes common to operate within this system or to falsify information in order to receive benefits.

In our nation, a child should never suffer from lack or malnutrition. Allow your child to experience a life other than one of poverty. I absolutely want for you and your children to be abundantly blessed. The Bible says, "Beloved, I pray that in every way you may succeed and prosper and be in good health (physically), just as (I know) your soul prospers (spiritually)." (3 John 1:2 AMP).

Anyone may encounter a low season in life and need to seek help through government programs and nonprofit organizations. However, we must be mindful not to cheat or steal from a system that was created for a temporary hand up. I experienced several crises during my childhood and faced difficulty when I was in college.

I want you to know that your circumstance can change, and your outcome can be different.

I want it to change for you so that it will change for your children. I sincerely want your children to have an abundant future.

This is my prayer for your family:

> Almighty God, I pray for this family. I ask You to change the way they believe. Father, I ask You to break poverty off their lives right now, in Jesus' name.
>
> I pray for them to seek You for forgiveness for every wrong decision they have ever made. I ask You to forgive them of all theft that they have ever committed. I ask You to give them understanding of their present conditions and knowledge to change their situations. I pray for them to trust You with the process of defeating poverty and lack in their homes, in Jesus' name. I ask You to create opportunities for them to prosper. In the name of Jesus, I command a

blessing in their lives and over their homes. Father God, I pray for them to be trustworthy in all things.

I ask You to break every curse, which has come through the generations, off their lives, in the name of Jesus. I ask that they no longer suffer for what family members have done—things that displeased You and caused a curse on their bloodlines—in Jesus' name.

I thank You for breaking and destroying the poverty that has been over their lives. I thank You for bringing revelation into their homes about You. I thank You for being God, our loving Father and sole provider, who sent Your son, Jesus, to earth to save and to redeem us. Thank You for empowering us with Your Holy Spirit. Amen.

Dear Mama, What Happened to Them?

So much has changed within our nation. There was a time when we respectfully honored the American flag, we boldly recited the "Pledge of Allegiance" and sang about the beauty of America.

I am disturbed when I see adolescents burning the American flag. I have watched news reports and have wondered where their parents are. I have wondered if anyone has told them about the many people who have died for this country to protect us. Many children's fathers were killed in wars. There are children without mothers. There are people without legs and arms. Others do not have eyes. Great numbers of people have been severely scarred. Many men and women cannot work because of mental scars and nightmares of war.

We are living the dream that so many people from other nations can only hope to have. A much-quoted scripture, which is read at military memorial services and funerals for the fallen soldiers, says, "Greater love has no one than this: than to lay down one's life for one's friends" (John 15:13 NKJV). The fallen laid down their lives for you, your children, your family, and our nation.

Dear Mama, Do Not Let My Daddy Hurt You

Domestic violence is all too common. Unfortunately, many children are in homes where constant domestic violence occurs. This atmosphere ignites fear in children. They can struggle with this fear into adulthood. Many children witness and are victims of their mom's boyfriend's violence.

Studies suggest that ten million children witness some form of domestic violence annually in the United States. It goes on to further say, men who witnessed their parents' domestic violence as children were twice as likely to abuse their own wives as opposed to sons of nonviolent parents[5].

Are your children aggressive toward their peers? Are they displaying the behavior they are witnessing around them? The National Domestic Violence Hotline will give assistance and essential information to adult and youth victims. The hotline is available twenty-four hours a day and seven days a week by calling 1-800-799-7233. If you reside outside of the United States, please refer to your country's assistance programs.

Divorce is possibly at its highest rate ever in our nation, and most families are blended families. God's hope is that a man and a woman would be joined together in the sanctity of marriage. The Bible says, "Therefore shall a man leave his father and his mother, and shall cleave unto his wife: and they shall be one flesh" (Genesis 2:24 KJV). Divorce destroys the family dynamic. It is my prayer that husbands and wives not give up on their marriages.

A 2015 research survey that followed reports and studies on marital stability and the protection from poverty since the early 1960s to the present says, "One of the most significant determinants, if not the most significant, of whether a man, woman or child live some large part of all of their lives in poverty, is the family from which they grow up in and those they go on to form, or fail to form, in their adulthood." This finding says that "there is an increasing knowledge that married mothers and fathers are a child's most potent protection from poverty, abuse, school failure, criminal behavior, and serious emotional problems"[6] (Stanton, 2015).

CHAPTER 6

Finishing Touches

———◦◦◦———

Good-Manners Are Not
Old-Fashioned

One of *Merriam-Webster*'s definitions for the
word manners is, "habitual conduct"[7]. This could
be synonymous with habitually; a habit of good
conduct or bad conduct. *Oxford English Dictionary*,
a British source, defines good manners as "polite

or well-bred social behavior"[8]. Some examples of this are, "Yes, ma'am," "No ma'am," "Please," and, "Thank you."

Politeness can always add polish to conversations. A child's life is enriched when an adult makes time to pour principles into him or her, such as appropriate behavior and good manners. Manners are not necessarily old-fashioned. I believe that good manners can be a doorway to countless opportunities throughout life.

My husband is a career soldier and a decorated veteran. As his spouse, I was well-groomed in the protocol of the United States Army by reading and becoming acquainted with the formality for the leadership; studying Army-spouse handbooks, and military manuals.

I am grateful that from childhood I was taught courteousness. I grew up in a demographic where respect toward adults was not a choice. I truly believe it has greatly benefited my life. I recall that when I was a little girl, I had teatime and treats, which were served on china by my godmother and adult god-sister during visits and overnight stays.

My godmother was an educator and was well known for her dignity. At times, I thought teatime was boring or a bit too elaborate. However, during our difficult family circumstances in our home, it was a great comfort. I have since enjoyed teatime with my own daughter and have lasting memories of giving her a catered high-noon tea party.

I have stood before many United States Army generals and colonels. I have also stood before leaders from the other branches of our military. We met numerous leaders of other allied and NATO countries and their spouses throughout my husband's career. I am grateful to have had the opportunity to serve others and to have honored and represented our country.

One of my most memorable opportunities

was when my husband and I were given the privilege of meeting Princess Anne, Queen Elizabeth of England's daughter. My husband was serving on a British/NATO staff and installation where we lived for nearly two and half years. I have fond memories of the British military protocol at that time.

We knew that we would be attending a major military event and our son's high school graduation ceremony on the same day. This required us to rush from one event to the other. At the outdoor ceremony, I was escorted to my assigned seating. From my seat, I was able to take pictures of Princess Anne on the parade field as well as her secret service detail. A lovely reception followed the ceremony; however, my mind was more concerned with strategizing on how to get home, change, and rush to our son's graduation.

At one point, I heard several whispers that Princess Anne had arrived at the reception.

They continued discussing her whereabouts and suggesting, Princess Anne was in the first ballroom at the reception. My husband and I were in our assigned area, which was nowhere near the princess. We were in an entirely different ballroom. We continued to talk with other guests until the British general of the installation brought Princess Anne over to meet us. There were many other people that he could have introduced her to, but God's favor shone on us. She had met others, but I strongly believe we were given the opportunity because the British general had examined our manners and behavior on many occasions. He trusted our conduct as well as our dedication and loyalty to my husband's military assignment. I must say that Princess Anne was lovely. She had the stature of her mother. It was indeed our pleasure to meet her. Princess Anne did not only say hello but was genuinely interested in our lives.

You never know who will call your name. Like Esther, I had been through a process of grooming. Esther was a young lady whose story is in the Bible. God prepared her to later save the Jewish people. She was selected to be a candidate for a queen. If selected, her husband would be a king who reigned over 127 areas of the world, from India to Ethiopia (see Esther 1:1 NKJV). Esther experienced twelve months of purification before she could stand before the king and be considered a candidate. For six months, she was purified with oil of myrrh, another six months with perfumes and additional preparations (see Esther 2:12 KJV).

This process could not be hurried. This process required a length of time to prepare Esther for the moment when she would be presented to the king. Without doubt, I believe that Esther was a beautiful young woman whom the king's detail felt had much potential. She would just need to be prepared for greatness and taught the appropriate behavior. The purification process for that palace was twelve months.

I have lived for quite some time and have learned that our timeline is not the same as God's timeline when it regards our preparation to be used by Him for a significant purpose. Preparation and purifying are cultivated by good and bad experiences in our lives, along with wise instruction, which is found in the Bible. Being nurtured by loved ones, dedicated mentors, and caring educators who will train and demonstrate acceptable behavior can influence our lives.

Dear Mama, Please Teach Me Good Hygiene

Your child should know how to brush his or her teeth, take a bath/shower daily, and use deodorant at the appropriate age. Encourage him or her to hydrate his or her body with lotion—if your child does not have allergies to certain ingredients. This will help your child establish personal responsibility for himself or herself. Teach and address the importance of maintaining his or her hair. This includes haircuts for boys and styling for girls. Completing these tasks daily will inspire discipline and boost his or her confidence and self-worth. The availability of clean, pressed clothing each day demonstrates the importance of preparing for each new day.

CHAPTER 7

Legacy

———◆———

I believe that God has entrusted me to impart authentic kingdom living, and the tenacity of noncompromising character and morals into our own children, their generation, and the generations that will follow. I feel connected to Timothy, the Apostle Paul's son in the faith. I am a servant who does not think she is qualified to preach the gospel of Jesus Christ.

As I have grown over the years in my faith and matured as a mother, I have found myself referencing Timothy's mother and grandmother. The few words that have been about them have sparked intrigue in me. The Apostle Paul said, "When I call to remembrance the unfeigned [unfeigned means sincere] faith in thy grandmother Lois, and thy mother Eunice, and I am persuaded that in thee also" (2 Timothy 1:5 KJV).

What does the word *sincere* mean? *Merriam-Webster* says that it is synonymous with "wholehearted, heartfelt, and hearty and means genuine in feeling." It goes on to say that the meaning of the word *sincere* stresses the "absence of hypocrisy, feigning, or any falsifying embellishment or exaggeration."[9] The word *wholehearted* suggests "sincerity and earnest devotion without reservation or misgiving."[10]

The word *heartfelt* suggests "depth of genuine feeling expressed outwardly."[11]

Could it be that Lois' and Eunice's faith in God was so genuine that it was displayed in their everyday lives and the lives they touched as servants, or merely the light of God shining in very dark environments? Maybe, they were known throughout Lystra, where they lived, all the way up to Iconium (see Acts 16:1–2 NKJV) because they believed in a God that others could not see, as they studied the Word of God. Then they taught Timothy all they knew about the scriptures.

In the New Testament it says that after meeting the Apostle Paul, Timothy was led to Jesus Christ and then spread the gospel of Jesus Christ long after his ascension. The Apostle Paul recognized how Timothy's mother, Lois, and grandmother, Eunice, had raised him with sound devotion to godliness. These two women in the scriptures were remarkable.

When our children were very young and I was developing an intentional relationship with Jesus (not the religious one I knew from my youth), I would tell them that the inheritance I was going to leave them was the Word of God. As I learned, I taught them. I wanted them to develop a relationship with Jesus that would be with them throughout their lives. Our son has shared with me how he remembers my transformation.

I am hopeful that my life has invoked a legacy and that every generation after me will live in the holiness of God. I claim generations of Eunices, Loises, and Timothys. I pray that our daughter will be a Lois and our son will be a Timothy. I pray this for their children and their children's children also. I have the faith to believe it for my children and your children. Psalm 78:3–7 says,

> "Which we have heard and known,
> and our fathers have told us. We will

not hide them from their children, telling to the generation to come the praises of the Lord, and his strength, and his wonderful works that he has done. For he established a testimony in Jacob, and appointed a law in Israel, which he commanded our fathers, that they should make them known to their children: That the generation to come might know them, the children who would be born; that they may arise and declare them to their children, that they may set their hope in God, and not forget the works of God, but keep His commandments". (NKJV)

NOTES

1 Oxford English Dictionary, accessed July 2017, https://oed.com.

2 Oxford English Dictionary, accessed July 2017, https://oed.com.

3 Study of Slumbering babies, University of Colorado, Boulder, May 10, 2017, lead author Phillip Gilley, PhD; principal investigator of the Neurodynamic laboratory at the Institute of Cognitive Science (ISC);

co-authors Kristin Uhler, assistant professor, CU Anschutz School of Medicine; Kaylee Watson, doctor of Audiology candidate CU Boulder department of Speech, language, and hearing sciences; Christine Yoshinaga-Itano, professor with ICS, accessed July 2017, https://www.colorado.edu/today/2017/05/10

4 Office of Juvenile Justice and Delinquency Prevention (OJJDP), accessed 2019, https://ojjdp.ojp.gov

5 Domestic Violence Statistics, accessed July 2018, https://domesticviolencestatistics.org.

6 Family in America, A Journal of Public Policy, published Fall 2015, author Glenn T. Stanton, director of Global Family Formation Studies on the Family, accessed July 2018, https://familyinamerica.org.

7 Merriam Webster Dictionary online, accessed July 2018, https://merriam-webster.com/dictionary.

8 Oxford English Dictionary, accessed July 2018, https://oed.com.

9 Merriam Webster Dictionary online, accessed July 2018, https://merriam-webster.com/dictionary.

10 Merriam Webster Dictionary online, accessed July 2018, https://merriam-webster.com/dictionary.

11 Merriam Webster Dictionary online, accessed July 2018, https://merriam-webster.com/dictionary.

ABOUT THE AUTHOR

During her husband's military career, Tonia served as a Vacation Bible School, children's church, and substitute teacher. Additionally, she was an educational assistant, parent volunteer, extracurricular activity volunteer, and a school advisory council president for two terms. Tonia also taught college-level, skill-requirement courses for Army Soldiers while simultaneously serving in various military spouse leadership positions.

As a senior spouse advisor and throughout her husband's career, Tonia was recognized for her steadfast service to Soldiers and their families with numerous Department of the Army awards, in addition to many other military spouse awards. She often personally kept families informed during lengthy deployments and field exercises. Tonia's care for the well-being of family members often challenged her to plan regular activities and tours for them. She also worked as a quality-assurance evaluator with the Department of Defense Dependents Schools, Europe (DoDDs-E). Tonia is an ordained minister.

Printed in the United States
By Bookmasters